Let's Discuss

OLD AGE

Roger Halls

Let's Discuss

First published in 1988 by
Wayland (Publishers) Limited
61 Western Road, Hove
East Sussex BN3 1JD, England

Editor: Elizabeth Clark
Designer: David Armitage

**British Library Cataloguing in
Publication Data**
Halls, Roger
    Let's discuss old age.—(Let's discuss)
    1. Old age
    I. Title   II. Series
    305.2'6

ISBN 1-85210-441-4

Typeset, printed and bound
in the UK at
The Bath Press, Avon

Front cover: *Looking on the bright side.
But do pensioners have a fair deal?*

Contents

The case studies in this book are fictitious. They are not subject to copyright and may be reproduced for use in the classroom.

What is Old Age?

In the UK there are almost 10 million people over retirement age. This is 17.3 per cent of the total population. Two thirds are women.

However, it is difficult to define old age. In the UK women receive a state old-age pension at 60, men being eligible five years later at 65. As life expectancy grows, many people can look forward to surviving into their 80s and 90s. Is it possible to classify everyone between 60 and 90 plus as simply being 'old'? There are enormous differences between individuals in such an age range.

Perhaps the most common idea people have when they speak of 'old age' is that as we grow older our minds and bodies begin to wear out. There seems to be a biological clock which ensures that we grow, develop, age and then die. In some ways this is good because it means that youth and strength must constantly be introduced into the human race; that our species continues to evolve; and that weaker members are not left to help consume society's limited resources.

One image of old age. The Declaration of Human Rights states 'Everyone has the right to security in the event of unemployment, sickness, disability, widowhood, old age or other lack of livelihood in circumstances beyond his control.' How far are the old in our society treated in accordance with this Declaration?

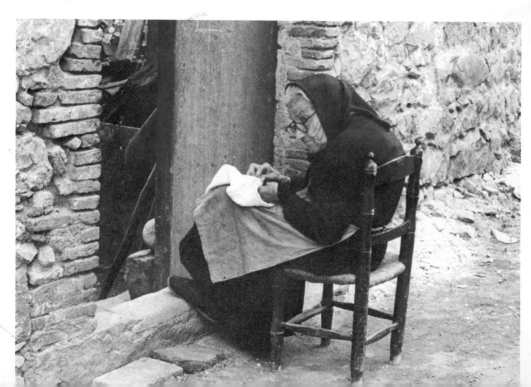

Sixty years of life experience take their toll. The same man in his twenties and in his eighties, showing the effects of the ageing process.

Generally speaking, normal ageing is shown by the greying and thinning of the hair. The organs of sense are commonly affected with wrinkling of the skin, the sinking of the eyes and the drooping of the eyelids. Lack of elasticity in the lens of the eye and the inner ear lead to deteriorating sight and hearing. Taste buds sensitive to sweetness and saltiness die off first, leaving old people increasingly sensitive to bitter and sour tastes in the food they eat. Other indications of ageing are a slackening of muscles and brittleness of bones.

However, all people are different and retain their faculties to varying ages. Some people at 80 are still walking, swimming, learning and so on. Others at 60 may, in comparison, be less physically and mentally active.

The effects of ageing, or of simply being classified as 'old', can be great. Contacts with friends and relatives become fewer. This may be caused by physical disabilities, making it more difficult for the elderly to travel. Isolation increases as people die, leaving alive fewer of one's own generation. Loneliness can be an unpleasant fact of life for the elderly.

Loss of work and the position it once gave can make people feel unimportant and believe they have nothing to contribute. To be thought and spoken of as 'old' or 'retired', particularly by the young, can make people feel irrelevant to what is going on around them and no longer part of what was once a world full of interest.

For many, however, old age can be a period of fruition. There is more time to relax and enjoy one's children and grandchildren. Old hobbies may be pursued and developed. New interests, such as helping in voluntary societies, may be taken up.

This feeling of fruition, found by some in Western industrial society, has long been the experience of the majority of the old in more traditional societies. In China and India the elderly are regarded as sources of wisdom and knowledge. They are respected because of their age, not in spite of it.

Life can be very lonely when the family has left home and only memories of the past remain.

This Russian patriarch is treated by his grandchildren with the respect traditionally given to the elderly in his society.

In most Western states, provision of an old-age pension guarantees the elderly some measure of independence. In Greece the old are still treated with great respect, but there are as yet no automatic pension rights for all. This means that much of the older generation is often dependent upon the younger for the necessities of life.

In most developing countries the problems involved in creating pensions schemes are very difficult, if not impossible, to solve. One reason is that pensions can only be paid from the wealth made by the countries concerned, and they cannot afford to do this. Another reason is that the numbers of old people are increasing too rapidly. By the year 2000, countries with high birth rates, such as Kenya with 53 births per 1,000 per year, will have very large proportions of their populations in the older range. In Latin America between 1970 and 2000 the numbers of the over 80s will have grown by 215 per cent.

In contrast France, a typical Western industrial state, has a birth rate of only fourteen per 1,000 per year. But even the present low birth rate in the West does create problems when combined with a continuously increasing survival rate. Since the beginnings of the Industrial Revolution in the eighteenth century, life expectancy in the UK has risen from 45 to 75 years. This is due, among other things, to the growth of medicine, the development of sanitation and generally improved living conditions. In the UK this has led to an increase of the over 65s from 4.7 per cent in 1900 to 14.7 per cent in 1980 as a percentage of total population. This continuing increase, combined with the current low birth rate, means that the share per child of tending aged parents will increase well into the next century.

Too old—or an invaluable source of wisdom and experience? This picture, taken in the House of Lords, shows the traditional dominance of elderly people in the chamber.

1 *Do you think old people deserve more respect in the UK than they are given?*
2 *Why is it, when the average age of the working population is falling, that old men still hold the top jobs as judges and dominate the House of Lords?*
3 *Why do old people in less developed countries look forward to having many grandchildren?*

Caring For and Helping the Old

Old people often need help in coping with the demands of daily living. Assistance with such tasks as cleaning the house, shopping, and tending the garden is sometimes essential if they are to continue leading a reasonably independent life. However, the elderly have social and psychological needs as well as physical ones.

Wider human contacts are needed in order to combat the feelings of isolation which often accompany old age. The simple act of giving a lift to the local library or to the home of an old friend can help an older, non-mobile person feel that he or she is still part of the community. Such a feeling is very important and can also have a beneficial effect upon that person's physical health.

The best and most effective help for the elderly is that which assists them in remaining independent and, as far as possible, keeping control of their own lives in their own homes. Providing specialized equipment such as grab handles to assist people in and out of the bath, or a wheelchair lift to

Maintaining frequent contact with friends is an important factor in avoiding feelings of isolation, a problem sometimes experienced by older members of society.

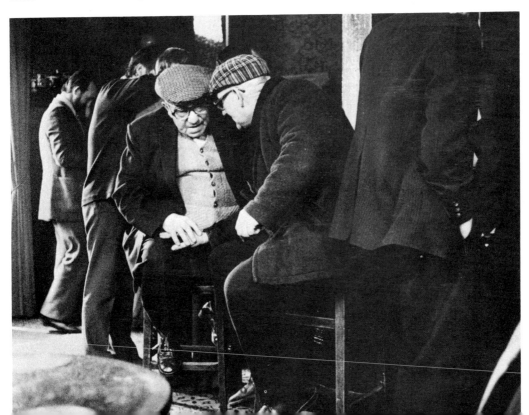

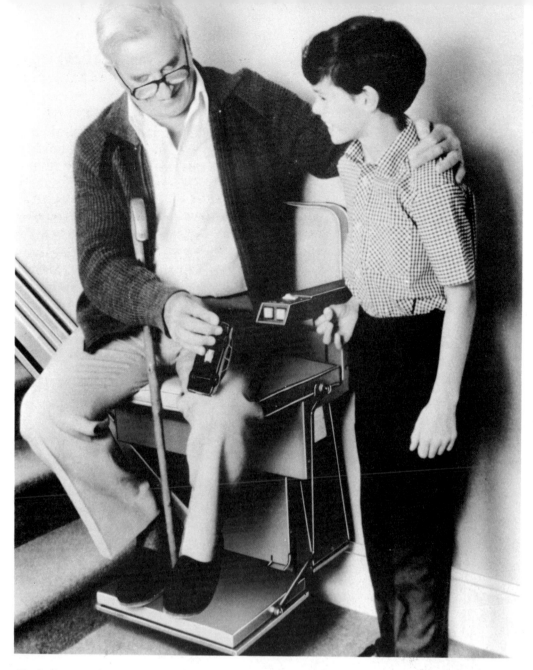

Gadgets such as a stairlift will often help a disabled person to remain independent and continue to live in his or her own home.

take them upstairs, can make all the difference between living independently at home and going into some kind of care.

The individuals and organizations helping the aged are many and varied. The most obvious are a person's own family, particularly children. This usually works well if the relatives live nearby. Unfortunately, young families today frequently have to move away because of the demands of work.

The older generation often prefer to remain in the place where they have always lived. It then becomes increasingly difficult to visit elderly parents who may now be a long way off.

Local friends and neighbours often help fill this gap. People one has known or worked with for many years, and who probably experience similar problems themselves, are usually only too happy to assist. For this reason it can often be unwise for people at retirement age to leave their home areas and live in a place where they do not know anyone.

The third group of those who help look after the interests of older people are those working for local voluntary organizations. Among these are the Women's Royal Voluntary Service (WRVS), Age Concern and Help the Aged. They often co-operate very closely with a fourth 'official' group: the National Health Service (NHS) and Social Services.

Both of these last two have legal obligations to provide certain amenities, not only for the old. They are run by central and local government. Social Services provide, among other things, facilities such as home help, mobile meals, an occupational therapy service and residential homes.

One function of the NHS is to provide people such as community nursing sisters (formerly known as district nurses) who dress wounds, give injections and generally look after the medical and psychological wellbeing of the old in their own homes. NHS health visitors give guidance, advice and instruction in health education matters. They advise on diet, safety in the home and, in co-operation with the Social Services, generally help supervize the frail and the vulnerable.

This WRVS volunteer, delivering Meals on Wheels, is one of the growing number of men working for the organization.

Many organizations provide transport to take the elderly on social outings and help them to attend such places as libraries and hospitals.

The voluntary organizations, mentioned earlier, work closely with these official bodies, which in turn often provide them with financial help. A good example of this co-operation is the Meals on Wheels service. It began with the war work of the WVS (the 'R' for 'Royal' was added recently), and local authorities have increasingly given it assistance. These subsidized meals provided for the old, sick and needy in their homes, have increased from 300,000 annually in 1947 to over 25 million annually over 40 years later.

Luncheon clubs for old people, often run jointly by voluntary organizations and Social Services, have grown to over 4,000 in number since starting in 1970. There are also day care centres where social contacts may be made. These are helpful both for old people and for their families, who may need relief from the stress imposed by caring for the elderly.

Many other types of voluntarily-run centres for the retired operate ambitious social and educational programmes ranging from ballroom dancing to art classes.

Voluntary groups such as Age Concern and Help the Aged have pioneered schemes to bring such things as chiropody services into the home. They work at providing meal services and starting good neighbour schemes to promote local self-help among old people. One of their most important areas of work lies in providing pensioners with information about legal rights and how to claim their proper entitlement from the state. They have also encouraged the development of 'Task Force' groups of young people, who volunteer to work for the elderly on such activities as decorating, gardening and shopping. In this way the older and younger generations have been brought close together in many areas of the country, and the isolation of many elderly people has been at least partly broken down.

Young 'Task Force' volunteers help bridge the gap between the generations by offering help and companionship to elderly people.

Case Study 1:

Mary, aged 70

In 1982 Mary and her husband Jack were both 64. They had been happily married for 40 years and were looking forward to Jack's retirement, when he died unexpectedly of a sudden and massive heartattack.

Mary was grief-stricken. As her son Malcolm, who lives in Canada, said at the time 'Mum never had many interests outside the family home and she just doesn't know how to cope.' Although still fit for her age, Mary began to find it difficult to take any interest in shopping and housework. She increasingly shut herself away in her home, began to eat very poorly, and refused to go out to meet any of her old friends.

Neighbours tried to help by offering to take her out for day trips and by inviting her round to their houses for coffee and a chat. None of this worked and she even refused Malcolm's invitation to visit him in Canada to meet her grandchildren.

All efforts failed until Ada, Mary's friend next door, upset at seeing how thin Mary was becoming, insisted they went together to the local luncheon club for the retired.

From then on things improved greatly. 'I realized I was becoming too full of self-pity and not thinking of others,' says Mary. 'Some of the people I began to meet were much worse off than I was. Many couldn't even get out of the house to do shopping unless they were taken by car. So I decided to volunteer to do some driving for the Day Centre in town.

'Hardly a day goes by when I'm not off somewhere with people in the car. I must admit I've never met so many people in my life before!

'I've even been persuaded to start a needlework group at the centre for the retired. The funny thing is that I seem to have more energy to do things now than I had even when Jack was alive. Perhaps I made the mistake then of leaving all the decisions to him.'

A luncheon club, run by the Social Services and a voluntary organization, offers social contact as well as inexpensive meals. Such a club can help to give its members a new interest in life.

1 What difficulties can you foresee in caring for an elderly relative living in the next street?
2 Does the work of the official and unofficial caring organizations weaken people's feelings of responsibility for elderly members of the family?

'At 70, all people should be put into homes for the elderly. This would remove a burden from the young and provide the old with plenty of company.' Discuss this view.

Where to Live

In the UK 89 per cent of old age pensioners live in private accommodation, 5 per cent in sheltered accommodation, and 6 per cent in residential homes or hospitals.

Perhaps the best place for old people to live is in their own homes. In that way they can decide for themselves how they arrange their own day; choose what they want to eat; go out and return when it pleases them, and so on. In some city areas old people are encouraged to fit visible alarm systems in windows overlooking the street so they may call for help in an emergency. This gives them confidence to continue their normal lives.

Problems often arise when elderly parents move in with their children. The difficulties are not so great if a 'granny flat' is available in the same house, because old people do not then feel 'in the way'. They know that company is nearby and they will be helped quickly in an emergency.

Elderly people living with younger family members often have to adapt in order to fit in and be accepted. It can be difficult sometimes for them to adjust to a new, often subordinate, role when they have been accustomed to dominating.

Sheltered accommodation can provide independence combined with security. It also has the advantage of giving people living on their own access to companionship and friendship with neighbours of similar ages and interests.

However, family strains can be caused by the different generations living closely together. If an old person needs a lot of attention it can cause resentment in the person who has to provide the care—usually a daughter or daughter-in-law. In turn, guilty feelings often arise within the carer because of this resentment, which is felt to be a sign of selfishness and ingratitude.

A wife or husband showing great concern for an aged parent can also arouse jealousy within the other marriage partner, who may no longer feel the centre of affection.

The pressures upon the elderly in this situation are also great. They may feel obliged to keep out of the way, or to make themselves acceptable by attempting to be uncomplaining, good-humoured, and helpful. The latter can often have disastrous results. Some old people, on the other hand, are unable to forget the authority they once had over their now adult children. This can make them critical and domineering, particularly if they feel choice and independence are being removed 'for their own good'.

But despite the problems, most families do still seem to feel responsible for their older members. A recent study of old people in London showed that if they had children still alive they were far less likely to find themselves in hospitals, geriatric wards or residential homes than people who did not have children living.

'Sheltered accommodation' is a solution which combines the above advantages of living independently with those of having company and assistance. Such assistance may be provided by private or charitable trusts, or by a local authority. Under this arrangement, several small flats, bed-sits or bungalows are grouped together on one site with a warden in overall charge. There may also be facilities such as laundrettes and common-rooms where people can meet.

The advantages are that the elderly retain their independence but can rely upon the nearby warden who is able to deal with problems caused by illness or accident. In addition, larger houses are freed for family use and the elderly are kept out of institutions.

One disadvantage is that wardens can become overworked as the residents become older and need more care. It can be difficult to persuade the sick and feeble to move out of such accommodation, particularly if it is owned by the tenants themselves and not rented. It is also difficult to keep an age balance between the 'young old' and the 'elderly old'.

There are other ways for the old to remain independent. Charitable groups such as the Abbeyfield Association own large old houses which are divided into bed-sitters. An applicant may then buy one of these. Many such places provide a housekeeper, who also prepares the main meals.

It is comforting for elderly people in sheltered accommodation to know that a warden is available to give help in an emergency.

The well-equipped lounge of a modern long-stay wing for the elderly in a NHS hospital.

For people unable to look after themselves there are places in residential care and in hospitals. Most of the 6 per cent of retired people in this group live in public or private homes for the elderly. The best are happy places, but the worst are full of people waiting to die. In the late 1980s there are about 6,000 of these homes in England and Wales. Approximately 85 per cent of the places in them are provided by local authorities. Such care can be expensive and often lacking in privacy.

Old people needing constant attention are provided for in nursing homes, geriatric wings in large general hospitals, and in smaller more specialized hospitals.

The elderly impose a heavy burden on the health and social services in many areas. In some parts of the UK—mainly the seaside resorts of the South Coast, East Anglia, North Wales and Lancashire—pensioners make up more than a quarter of the population. In Worthing, 35 per cent of the population has reached retirement age. Many people have moved there from large industrial towns, remembering the happy holidays they spent at the seaside when they were children, or hoping for a friendlier climate.

Some go further afield for cheaper living and guaranteed sunshine to places such as mainland Spain, Majorca and the Canary Islands. However, isolation, a growing crime rate, and inflation abroad have led many to return to the UK.

Case Study 2:

Mr Green, aged 78

Mr Green spent all his working life in the Civil Service in London, retiring with a small pension in the mid 1970s. His wife Jane died in a car accident soon after they went to live in Worthing. Mr Green tried to struggle on by himself but his only daughter Helen insisted that he live with her and the family in Nottingham.

The arrangement worked very well for a few years until Mr Green suffered a stroke, which left him incontinent and partially paralysed. As a result, Helen was forced to give up her part-time job as a doctor's receptionist in order to look after her father.

Her husband John was sympathetic at first, but soon realized that the loss of income meant household economies were necessary if the mortgage were to be repaid. John become increasingly difficult to live with because of money worries. His wife and two children were very critical of him because of his bad temper.

Family rows became frequent, the children siding with their mother and grandfather when John suggested that the old man should be put into a residential nursing home.

'My father may be difficult to look after, but I love him and I'm not going to kick him out to live among strangers,' says Helen.

Crisis point came one evening during dinner at the family home. John had invited his boss and wife from the computer firm he worked for. He was keen to create a good impression.

Unfortunately, Mr Green, who had been put to bed before the guests arrived, came downstairs in his pyjamas during the meal. He began to ramble about computers in the Civil Service. After considerable embarrassment the old man was taken back to bed.

Later that night he wandered out of the house and caused a minor accident on the nearby main road as he strayed across it at midnight.

After that, even Helen admitted that her father ought to go into care. But they have no money to instal him in a private nursing home.

Sometimes residential nursing homes provide an atmosphere lacking in active stimulus for the residents. This can lead to boredom, social withdrawal and, sadly, a loss of interest in life.

1 Should public money be paid to private nursing homes for them to look after old people, or should the state provide all such nursing homes?
2 Imagine you are (a) Mr Green's daughter Helen and (b) John, her husband. Work out in turn your thoughts and feelings on the problem of Mr Green.
3 Where would you prefer to live in old age if you were healthy and single? Give your reasons.

Positive Aspects of Old Age

It is important to realize that after reaching the retirement age of 65 or 60 in the UK, men and women can quite easily still have between 20 per cent and 30 per cent of their lives left to live. If, as happens increasingly, people retire from their regular jobs at 50 plus, the proportion of non-working life left can grow still further to around 35–40 per cent. This move towards earlier job retirement could be a good thing, because it will mean people have more active years in front of them than used to be the case. It will also free more jobs for the young.

The fact that people live increasingly to greater ages means that an enormous leisured class has come into being—the elderly and retired. This class is more skilled, literate, articulate and informed than it was only twenty years ago.

Today, people are surviving to even greater ages. Here, John Evans, 110 years old, is presented with a certificate as Britain's oldest man in 1987.

Pablo Picasso still at work in his seventies. Insight and great creativity often continue into old age.

These people uncommitted to regular work could be a great asset to the UK if encouraged in a positive way. The difficulty is that the old are usually looked upon as a problem rather than an asset. There are increasing numbers of people who feel that this outlook must change. Many of the most powerful and influential people this century have contributed greatly when well-advanced in years. Winston Churchill (1874–1965) was Britain's war-time leader when he was an old-age pensioner. Pablo Picasso (1881–1973) was one of the most influential artists the world has ever seen. He was still working and developing his art shortly before he died in his nineties. Arthur Rubenstein, the great pianist, was performing in public well into his eighties. Bertrand Russell the philosopher influenced and led people over 60 years his junior during his work for world peace and co-operation. There are many examples of such well-known older figures being active well past retirement age.

Not all elderly people, though, will be able to contribute on such a grand scale. But most can give something as a result of a lifetime's experience.

It is important to 'keep going' and not give in before necessary by regarding oneself as 'old'. Healthy, regular exercise and a good diet help prolong life and vigour, giving the physical and mental fitness which is so important with advancing years. A good example of such fitness is the adventurous Duchess of Arran who, in her 70s, is still pursuing her hobby of competitive power-boat racing.

The largest age group of voluntary helpers in organizations such as Oxfam, the Citizens Advice Bureau, the Council for the Protection of Rural England and so on, is that of the over-65s. These people are often sharing skills which they have developed over a lifetime of work.

Old people can also have a lot to offer on a more personal level within their own families. Grandparents are often very close to their grandchildren, and are a source of family history and tradition which cannot be replaced once it has been forgotten. The strength of early memory is surprising, even in elderly people who seem forgetful in ordinary day-to-day matters. The oldest members of a family contribute to family life in many other ways. Chief amongst them is listening to the aims, ambitions and problems of their children's children. They have more time to listen than the busy parents, who are often more concerned with earning a living in order to support the family. They also contribute by baby-sitting and helping out in any problem situations.

There are many courses available which encourage the elderly to keep active. A group of retired people watch closely as one of their members learns to ward off an attack during a self-defence class, a course aiming to promote fitness and security.

Providing the mind with new challenges and interests can actually slow down mental decline in the old. The stimulus offered by this French class at a day centre in Camden, keeps its students mentally alert.

The extra time available at an advanced age can be used to extend one's knowledge and mental abilities. Such ideas have only recently come to be more widely accepted than they were even a few years ago. Until recently it was thought that mental powers inevitably declined rapidly with age. This was put down to the dying of millions of brain cells as people became older. However, recent research around the world has shown that this mental decline can be slowed down, or even halted, in old people. The key lies in constant mental exercise.

In Queensland, Australia, 80 people between the ages of 63 and 91 were recently given weekly German lessons. After three months, half of them passed an examination normally taken by schoolchildren who had been studying German for three years. There are also impressive examples of very old people taking university degrees.

Physical decline can also be halted in old age. A long term experiment in the Soviet Union in the 1960s and '70s put 22 volunteers between 51–75 through a regular exercise programme. After ten years the volunteers were tested. They had the same average levels of strength and fitness as they had when they started.

Great physical and mental decline is not, therefore, inevitable for everyone in old age. But a positive outlook is all-important in realizing potential, and this is something that all older people should be encouraged and even educated to adopt in their attitudes toward themselves.

Case Study 3:

Benjamin and Louise, both aged 70

Benjamin and Louise are both 70 years old and have been happily married for over 40 years. After teaching architecture and art respectively at a London college for 25 years, they retired in their 50s and opened an antiques business. This was a great success and they are now comfortably well-off, having recently sold the business. They intend to retire to Cornwall where they will pursue their hobbies of painting and carpentry.

Their son Tom works in Australia as a geologist for a mining company. He recently asked his parents to visit him and his family for three months. Benjamin and Louise accepted.

However, ten days before they were due to fly out to begin their visit their daughter Catherine was taken ill and had to undergo a serious operation. She was told she would be unable to work or look after the family home in Worcester for at least six weeks. Louise discovered that her daughter was extremely worried about this.

'Catherine was concerned because her stay in hospital would mean that her husband, Charles, would have to look after the kids and give up an opportunity to go on a working trip to the Isle of Wight where he hoped to build up a new business. He had recently been made redundant from his job and so this trip was very important. If he missed it, he felt that his chances were pretty slim of finding another similar job and that he would have to go on Social Security.'

Fortunately, Benjamin and Louise were eager to help and postponed their Australian trip to look after the house and children. As Benjamin said, 'The family comes before anything else.' They are now looking forward to Catherine's return from hospital in two weeks' time.

Their three grandchildren have enjoyed the visit. 'Mum and Dad are O.K.,' said Simon, the eldest, 'but it's lots more fun when Gran and Grandad come to look after us.'

Many couples enjoy a happy retirement together, free from the earlier cares imposed by work and bringing up a family. This can be a very fruitful time.

1   Do you think it is good that elderly people run so many of Britain's voluntary associations?
2   Why, do you think, is it often the case that young people feel closer to their grandparents than to their parents?
3   What else can be done to give an interest in life to the many old people who feel bored by life during retirement?
4   Doctors are allowed to work past normal retirement age. Do you think this age should be fixed at 65?

Policy and Attitudes

In 1889 Germany introduced the world's first old age pension schemes and New Zealand followed in 1904. The UK started in 1908 with pensions for all citizens over 70. This was lowered in the 1930s to the present 65 for men and 60 for women. Many people say the qualifying ages should be equalized at 60. To do so, however, would mean spending more than £2,500 million extra per year.

British pensions are among the lowest in Europe. In 1985 the full French pension was 50 per cent of national average earnings, with a weekly minimum of £49.22. In the UK the corresponding figures were approximately 25 per cent, with a weekly maximum of £35.80. These figures have risen slightly since then, but the relative gap remains the same.

Since 1980 pensioners' living standards have fallen in the UK. Before that year, basic pensions were linked either to the forecast annual increase in price rises or to that of average earnings—whichever was the greater. This link was broken in 1980, from which year pensions were to be increased annually according to prices only. Because wages continued rising faster than prices, pensioners fell behind relative to workers. The pensioners' position has also worsened because a greater proportion of their income is spent on food and fuel, which rise in price more quickly than other goods.

Collecting the retirement pension is an important event of the week, but British pensions are gradually declining in value.

Norman Willis, general secretary of the TUC, with pensioners protesting against the reduced value of old age pensions at Westminster in 1986.

From 1983, pensions were no longer increased according to a forecast of price rises for the coming year, but according to the rises of the past year. Thus pensions never catch up with current inflation but always lag behind by about eighteen months. Between 1981–86, the above policies meant a loss for a couple of £573.80, and for a single person of £389.30.

The new Social Security Act of 1986 will also affect UK pensioners when it comes into full effect in 1988. For example, in 1987, 4.2 million retired people received Housing Benefit to help with rent and rates. The newly enforced Act will mean 2.7 million of them will receive less, and 250,000 will lose Housing Benefit altogether. This is caused by a new means test, which disallows help to anyone with more than £6,000 savings. In addition, pensioners who had all their rates paid for them will in future have to pay 20 per cent of them.

Another change under the Act is that from April 1988 single lump-sum payments for necessities such as bedding and house repairs will be abolished. The same applies to the Death Grant to assist with funeral expenses. Instead, a 'Social Fund' will make loans available. These will be made on the decision of DHSS staff and no appeal will be allowed against their rulings. No loans will be made to people with savings of more than £500.

It is claimed that loans will force pensioners to live in even greater poverty while paying them back. Poverty forces old people to economize on food and heating and risk hypothermia, and in 1984 the deaths of 857 people over 65, according to their death certificates, involved hypothermia. More people die annually of this condition in the UK than die of it in the whole of Scandinavia. However, no severe weather payments to help with heating will be paid to those with over £500 in savings. Such payments have to be applied for, and are paid after the bills have been settled. This causes much distress to many pensioners. Most other European nations seem to treat their elderly as a greater priority than is the case in Britain.

As a result of these policies, many groups have sprung up to work for the interests of pensioners. The National Federation of Old Age Pensions Associations, founded in 1939, has increased its membership to almost a million. The National Pensioners' Convention (founded by Jack Jones, the former General Secretary of one of the biggest trade unions in Britain, and himself a pensioner) is an umbrella organization for pensioners' groups and charities campaigning on behalf of the retired. It was founded to co-ordinate the work of these bodies in order to influence government policy by approaching local councillors and MPs. The Convention also meets with the Prime Minister and ministers connected with pensioners' welfare. Its current aim is for a basic pension set at one half of average earnings for a married couple and not less than a third for a single person.

Workers packing 'Cold Crisis' kits at the Age Concern Headquarters, to be distributed around the country to help the elderly combat the freezing winter weather. Each kit contains a fuel voucher, a thermal vest, a packet of soup, a tin of drinking chocolate and advice on keeping warm.

Jack Jones, the ex-trade union leader, now works for the interests of pensioners during his own retirement.

The difficulties caused by low pensions are probably made worse by the feeling pensioners have that much of society looks down upon them. Youth is fashionable, possibly as a result of young people becoming more affluent in the 1960s and '70s. Older, poorer people are thought of as almost irrelevant in a society where money and goods earn one respect.

The portrayal of old people in television and advertising as mainly decrepit, foolish and laughable is also very demoralizing for them.

These attitudes may change though, as a larger proportion of the UK population is made up of the elderly, and if unemployment among the young continues to be a feature of life.

On television, the old have often been presented as ridiculous and comic figures. Here Clive Dunn plays Jonesy in 'Dad's Army', famous for panicking and relating tedious stories about his past.

Case Study 4:

Elsie, aged 82

During the bitterly cold winter months of 1987, Elsie, aged 82, nearly died of hypothermia.

As her shocked nephew, Jim, explained 'She lives alone and refuses to leave her own house for a place in a residential home for the elderly. She's always been very independent and proud. She finds it difficult enough to make her pension stretch to cover food and heating in a normal winter. When the bitter weather struck, she felt she had to forego some warmth in order to keep the electricity bill down.

'She was entitled to a heating allowance, but she could not understand what she had to do to get it—it all seemed too complicated. I'm not sure that it would have been enough anyway. She could not bear being unable to pay a bill—something to do with her generation, I suppose.

'I was horrified by the news that she nearly died. I live about 160 km (100 miles) away and relied too much on neighbours to help. I'm her only surviving relative and I shall try to persuade her to go into care.'

A neighbour found Elsie. 'I just thought I'd pop in and see how she was doing. I'd shopped for her at the weekend and warned her to keep the heating on. Two days later, there she was huddled on her sofa totally unconscious and blue-lipped. The place was ice-cold. I rang the ambulance. She was taken to hospital and just pulled through. I really think she will have to go into care now.'

Elsie recounted in hospital, 'I lay on that sofa, covered up in blankets and sang to keep my spirits up. I felt very weak and knew I was slowing down. But I had to ration the amount of fuel I used. It was too much effort in the end to go and make something to eat or drink. I don't remember blacking out or the ambulance. I woke up in hospital and they told me I'd been a naughty girl for skimping on myself. But what could I do? I've always paid my way. I knew the heating bill would be enormous if I kept it on all day and I couldn't bear not being able to pay. I'll be more careful in future.'

Elsie was transferred to a local residential home where she is still very homesick.

1 What effect do you think the Social Security Act of 1986 will have upon old age pensioners?
2 In what ways are British pensioners not treated as well as those of many other EEC countries?
3 How would you wish to improve the position of pensioners in the UK?
4 What measures do you suggest could be taken to prevent elderly people living alone from becoming victims of hypothermia?

The elderly poor living alone spend a lot of time worrying about such things as fuel and food bills. Anxiety about 'making ends meet' can sometimes lead to dangerous self-neglect.

Problems Faced in Old Age

On retirement many people feel a loss of identity and status. At work they may have been in a position where they were used to leading others or giving orders. Now, because they have no recognized position, they have few or no responsibilities and very little authority. This applies especially to people who were once forces' personnel, policemen and women, teachers, nurses, industrial managers and so on. The loss of people's company at work can also be particularly depressing.

Retired people are often referred to as being 'ex' members of a profession or occupation. This can have the effect of making individuals feel they are no longer the people they used to be. A feeling of worthlessness can quickly follow. This idea is often made much worse by the fact of no longer being part of a large social group of friends and relations.

It is particularly difficult being made redundant a few years before retirement, as there are almost no jobs for people who are in this age range.

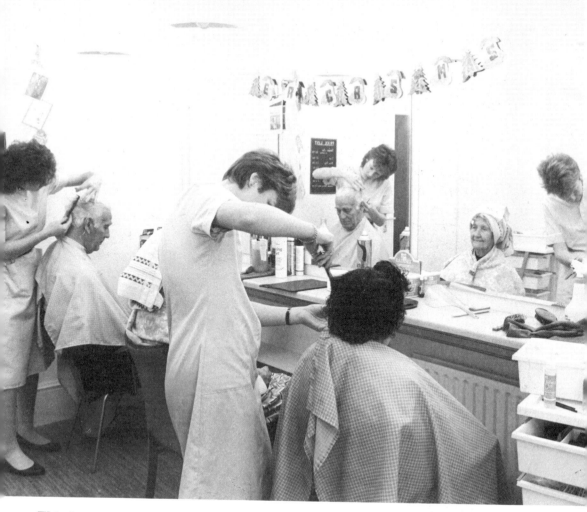

This low-cost hairdressing salon in a modern day centre helps people to retain self-respect by enabling them to take care of their appearance.

This group inevitably becomes smaller as the years pass and people die off. Children often move away, either to another area of the country or to a different part of the world. Isolation grows with advancing age.

Health and strength, if not worked at positively, usually decline as people grow older. One's good looks from youth begin to fade and this can be most distressing. The growing popularity of face-lifts shows that people do not lose their vanity as they age. Despite the claims made for certain substances that they will re-vitalize ageing bodies, there is no evidence to show the truth of these claims. Ginseng, a root from the Far East, and Vitamin E (used in many cosmetics) are growing in popularity and use among middle-aged and older people. Although expensive, they have not proven themselves to be effective in combating the effects of ageing.

As people grow feebler with age they become increasingly dependent upon the younger and fitter. They lose their ability to take their own decisions and often have to do what they are told by the people looking after them—often their own children, or staff in nursing homes and hospitals.

Feeling powerless, some old people imagine others are plotting to remove their independence. They can sometimes give way to what seems to be unreasonable anger, aggression, and refusal to co-operate. This is usually an expression of frustration and an attempt to reassert their past independence. People responsible for old people have to be patient and understanding at such times.

A warden of a sheltered housing scheme advises a resident on her medication.

At last, the opportunity to concentrate on a life-long interest or hobby. Old age can be a time of development too.

Old age hits most hard at those who have no hobbies, or whose hobbies—such as sport—were dependent upon physical strength and fitness. Many old people who still enjoy their lives say that one of the main things keeping up their interest is a physically undemanding hobby which they began when much younger. Activities such as photography, reading, needlework and painting can all be enjoyed to an advanced age.

It is a mistake to imagine that all older people will necessarily enjoy 'a well-earned rest' and a chance to 'put their feet up'. This quickly leads to boredom and a much earlier death than might otherwise be the case.

However, it is difficult to sustain an interest in life—even if one is fit and well—without a reasonable level of income. In the UK the elderly are, generally speaking, the poorest section of the population. They are the most likely to live in sub-standard housing and to lack hot water, indoor toilet, bathroom and central heating. Old people are less likely than other sections of the population to possess a fridge, washing machine and other domestic equipment. For many this is simply a continuation of lifelong underprivilege, but with age the situation becomes less easy to bear.

The usual sources of income for the old are the state old age pension and perhaps an occupational pension. At the present time the latter is confined mainly to men and the proportion of women who worked outside the home in pensionable occupations such as teaching, the medical profession, and the Civil Service. The position of widows and single women can be particularly difficult if they do not qualify for an occupational pension. Supplementary benefit is available if total income falls below a minimum. In the 1980s, over 20 per cent of all retired people qualified for this benefit.

This elderly man is typical of many pensioners, who, as a group, lack much of the equipment that most people take for granted.

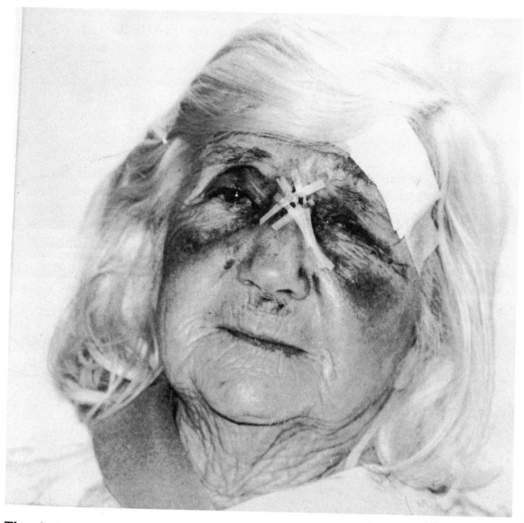

The disturbing increase in violent attacks on the elderly makes many old people virtual prisoners in their own homes. This partially blind 86-year-old woman suffered severe injuries when mugged in 1987.

There were other supplements payable for heating, special diets, physical disablement, laundry, rent and rate rebates, and many other needs. The problem was that the regulations governing such payments were often difficult to understand. One's rights were not easily discovered! The new 1986 Act will affect all these from 1988.

In addition to these difficulties, many able-bodied old people, particularly in inner city areas, are terrified of leaving their homes. This is because of the increasing chance of being attacked in the street, a new and distressing fact of modern life for old people. There has also been a disturbing rise in the number of attacks on the elderly in their own homes.

Case Study 5:

Ernest, aged 72

Ernest, an ex-police sergeant from Bradford, is 72 and bed-ridden. He feels this particularly badly as up to six months ago he had led an active outdoor life. He was a keen athlete in his younger days, representing his club at cross-country running. Although advanced in years, Ernest and his wife Madeline continued their outdoor pursuits well into their 70s. They were active members of the Ramblers Association and shared a keen interest in gardening and golf.

'Mum's death two years ago almost finished the old boy,' said his bachelor son Roy, with whom Ernest now lives. 'He seemed to lose interest in everything. Then he decided to sell up the house and came to live here in York with me.

'I'm not sure that was a good idea as he's always been a rather domineering man. He seemed to think I was still a little boy and tried to tell me what to do here in my own place. We had quite a few rows.

'One day, he had a fall on the stairs and broke his hip. They tried an operation at the hospital but it didn't really succeed, I'm afraid. He's in a lot of pain and has started to waste away physically. He seems to have given up hope. I've never seen him so depressed. The doctor thinks unless Dad makes a real mental effort he'll probably never walk again.

'A couple of weeks ago he said he'd rather be out of it all if he couldn't have a decent, active life. After that he began to ask me to give him an overdose of his sleeping pills and pain-killers to help him out of his misery.

'I really don't know what to do. I hate to see him like this—he's never had a day's illness before in his life. It's horrible to see him suffering and crying with the pain at times. One part of me says if I love him I should help him out of his misery. The other part says it would be murder. But then, it is possible that he might recover. I'm at my wits' end!'

This man may be a permanent invalid after a serious accident. The prospect of permanent confinement to bed as an invalid dependent on others often causes severe depression and loss of the will to live. Should people have the right to choose when to die?

1 Should all people undergo a compulsory training course to pre-
   pare them for retirement?
2 What in your opinion are the reasons for the growth in attacks
   upon old people by the young?
3 Should old people be able to choose the time to die? What difficulties do you see in a policy of voluntary euthanasia?

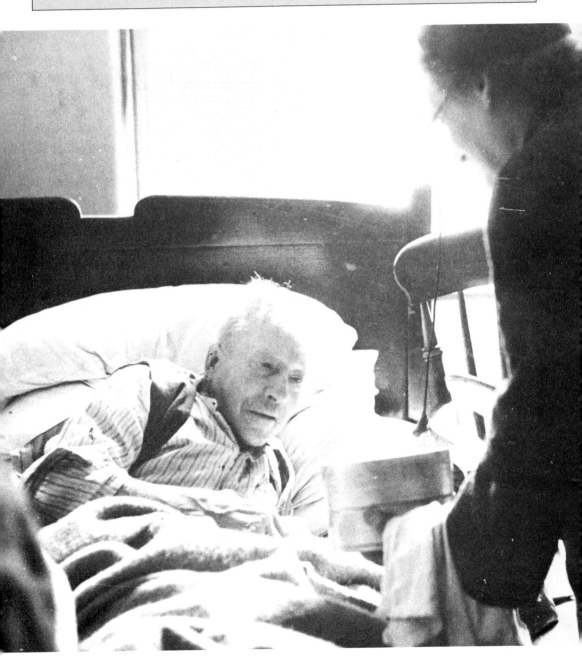

Outlook For Old People

Circumstances are changing for old people. In some ways, during the last 20 years, more notice has been taken of their needs. Much effort has been expended trying to cater for this section of the population.

The Open University (OU), which offers degree courses via television, radio and short courses, is becoming increasingly geared to catering for people of advanced years as well as the younger and middle-aged groups. Many people over retirement age have gained OU qualifications already.

Another most interesting development in higher education for old people has been the establishment of the 'University of the Third Age', or U3A for short. This idea began in Toulouse, France, in 1973 and the first British U3A was founded at Cambridge in 1982. The aim of the U3A movement is to encourage mental and physical activity and health among older people.

These institutions are very different from ordinary universities and not only because they cater solely for the retired. The first unusual thing about them is that no paper qualifications are required to gain entrance, and no qualifications are given by the universities to their students. The curriculum includes the usual academic subjects, plus leisure activities of all kinds, sports, and almost as many different hobbies as there are people studying.

An increasing number of retired people are taking up serious study for the first time in their lives, many taking degrees.

Social occasions where old and young mix contribute greatly to bringing the generations closer together.

There are no separate teaching members of staff at a U3A: no lecturers, professors or principals. Nor are there students in the generally accepted definition, for all teach and all are taught. All contributions are made by the elderly and retired people themselves and are drawn from their own past occupations, experience and wisdom. Teaching and learning are centred upon discussion groups. What happens in the way of content and organization is decided by the groups themselves. U3A has shown that a large proportion of retired people can retain mental and physical interest in life if they decide not to allow their abilities to fall into disuse.

Much of the present wide-spread attitude to ageing still needs to change, however, among young and old alike, despite the encouraging lead taken through movements such as U3A. It is still a fact that many younger people think of the elderly as a special category of quaint old souls a long way past all interesting activity. The idea of the sweet elderly couple, Darby and Joan, who are harmless and to be patted on the head and then forgotten, is still very strong. Many old people, also, are only too willing to accept this idea of themselves. Travel concessions on road and rail, together with firms specializing in holidays for the over 55s, all encourage the non-retired to think of old people as a special group who are different, and separate, from the general population.

There is an urgent need to bring elderly people back into the mainstream of general life. This is particularly true now that the proportion of old people in the UK is growing so rapidly. With a society becoming less based upon heavy industry and the need for demanding physical skills, older people may well be able to contribute more to economic life in the future.

A society based upon people providing services, and where goods are increasingly made by robots, may offer older people the chance to give of their experience and knowledge gained over a lifetime. Perhaps it will be possible to tap the reservoir of wit and wisdom among the old. To do this, the elderly must be interested in the future, while drawing upon their experience of the past. Such an attitude to life is shown by a group called the 'Seavets' based near Reading in Berkshire. They are a group of sport-loving old age pensioners who formed their own sail-boarding club. They have found a new pastime at a late age and are making a success of the challenge. The idea that elderly folk are fit only for ballroom dancing and looking back to the past is one which, many would say, has to go.

An elderly woman familiarizes herself with some 'new technology'. Old people often enjoy learning new skills.

An 80-year old windsurfer takes to the waves with a skill to be envied by many younger people.

Some people might object that it is not always possible for elderly people to take on such challenges. The fact that 40 per cent of the NHS budget is spent on the over 65s shows that health does decline with age, though much can be done to avoid the worst effects. Even so, lack of money, and an increasing dependence on others, will hold back many pensioners from improving their lives.

Indeed, some would argue that to push pensioners' power and influence may produce a kind of backlash among some members of the younger generation. In the USA, old people's pressure groups have gained an increasing social role for their members, but at the expense of what some critics would call the start of a war between the generations.

Some people are already asking whether this could happen in the UK.

1 What needs to be done to encourage the elderly to mix with younger generations?
2 Are there dangers in encouraging older people to increase their activity and influence?
3 Do you think the outlook for old people is encouraging or discouraging?

Glossary

Amenities Services, such as meals on wheels, libraries, and so on.

Articulate Skilful at expressing oneself in speech.

Chiropody Foot care and treatment.

DHSS Department of Health and Social Security.

Euthanasia Mercy killing, by bringing an easy death to the incurably sick.

Geriatric So physically and mentally enfeebled through age that full-time care is needed.

Hypothermia Condition caused by severe drop in normal body temperature.

Incontinent Unable to control the workings of the bladder and sometimes the bowels.

Inflation Rising prices.

Literate Able to read and write.

Means test An investigation to discover a person's financial means before any government help, if any, is given.

Occupational therapy Treatment given through developing a patient's manual skills.

OU Open University.

Psychological To do with the mind.

Stroke Sudden disabling attack caused by a brain haemorrhage (bleeding) often leaving the sufferer partially or totally paralysed.

Subsidized Supported by payments, usually from central or local government, to cover part of the costs of providing a service.

Further Reading

Non-fiction:

Attitudes Resource Kit (Age Concern, 1979)

Beyond Three Score and Ten by Mark Abrams (Age Concern, 1978, 1980)

Black and Asian Old People in Britain by Jonathan Barker (Age Concern, 1984)

Growing Older (HMSO, 1981)

Let's Get Moving by Eira Davies (Age Concern, 1975)

Fiction:

A Christmas Carol by Charles Dickens (Puffin Classics, 1984)

Celebrating Age: An Anthology by Ann Spokes-Symonds (Age Concern, 1987)

Marrying Off Mother by Christine Nostlinger (Andersen Press, 1984)

The Granny Project by Anne Fine (Methuen, 1983)

The Growing Pains of Adrian Mole by Sue Townsend (Methuen, 1984)

The Secret Diary of Adrian Mole Aged 13¾ by Sue Townsend (Methuen, 1982)

Videos:

Presenting An Image, in the series 'Media Studies: Looking Into Television' (BBC)

You can obtain useful factsheets on the subject of old age and the organizations set up to help the elderly from:

Age Concern
Bernard Sunley House
60 Pitcairn Road
MITCHAM
Surrey   CR4 3LL

Acknowledgements

The publishers would like to thank the following for providing the photographs in this book: Age Concern 13, 18, 27, 33, 36; Camera Press 8, 15, 24; Format Photographers 17, 21, 44; Roger Halls 5 (both), 11, 12, 19, 28, 31 (above), 34, 35, 42, 43; D. Henoud 4; Lisa Mackson 6; Network *cover*, 9, 25, 38; Popperfoto 7, 23, 37; Stannah Stairlift 10; Topham 16, 22, 29, 30, 31 (below), 39, 41, 45.

Index